Monographic Journals of the Near East　　　*Afroasiatic Linguistics* 8/2 (October 1982)

CENTRAL SOMALI—A GRAMMATICAL OUTL

by

John I. Saeed
School of Oriental and African Studies, London

There are three major dialect groups of Somali: Common (or Northern) Somali, Benaadir Somali, and Central Somali (Rahanwin, Af Maymay etc.). This article presents an outline of the Central Somali spoken in the Bay region of southern Somalia, including the city of Isha Baydhaba (Iscia Baidoa). Aspects of the dialect's phonology, morphology, and syntax are described and a sample English-Central Somali lexicon is provided. The study reveals that this dialect differs considerably from the other Somali dialects. It is also apparent from the description that this dialect is very similar indeed to that called Jabarti by Leo Reinisch and Maria von Tiling.

Table of Contents

1. INTRODUCTION

This article describes the Somali dialect spoken in and around the city of Isha Baydhaba[1] in Southern Somalia. According to its speakers it is very similar to that spoken in the town of Bur Hakaba, some sixty kilometers to the southeast. Research on this dialect was conducted over a period of several weeks with students from the Baydhaba area studying at Lafoole College, near Afgooye, about twenty-five kilometers west of Mogadishu. In addition the author was able to make brief trips to Isha Baydhaba and Bur Hakaba.

In this article the Somali dialect which is spoken in Somalia north of the Shabeelle River, in the Ogaden, in Jibouti, and by almost all Somalis in northeastern Kenya, is called Common Somali. This, the most prestigious of the dialects, has generally been used as a *lingua franca* among other dialects and, with some accomodation to the speech of Mogadishu, is now becoming the standard of the Somali Republic. It is also used by external sources such as the radio broadcasts in Somali from Nairobi, Addis Abeba, Cairo, Moscow, and London. Since it geographically surrounds other dialects, the term Northern Somali, by which it is sometimes known, is felt to be inappropriate and is not used here. The closely related dialect spoken in Mogadishu and the towns of the Benaadir coast will here be termed the Benaadir dialect. The apparently inter-related dialects spoken south of the Shabeelle River and inland from the Benaadir coast are termed Central Somali dialects, and it is with these that the present study is concerned.

The Baydhaba dialect is not mutually intelligible with either Common or Benaadir Somali. Its speakers recognize that a series of dialects related to their own spread from just behind the Benaadir coast, across Somalia south of the Shabeelle, to the Ogaden. They are bounded to the south, in Kenya, and to the east, in Ethiopia, by speakers of Common Somali. It is not possible to provide figures for the number of Central Somali speakers, but their area includes both extensive agricultural lands, which have a higher

---

[1]Often written on maps in the Italian form of *Iscia Baidoa*.

population density than much of Somalia, and also the major town of Baydhaba. The Italian census of 1931 gave the number of the Rahanwiin clan group, one of the major groups of Central Somali speakers, as 254,020 (Lewis 1955).

Very little has been written about these dialects of southern Somalia and the author is thus encouraged to present this material despite the tentative nature of much of the analysis. The Baydhaba dialect is obviously very closely related to the dialect called Jabarti by Reinisch (1904) and von Tiling (1921, 1924). There is also great similarity, though to a lesser extent, between this dialect and Moreno's Digil (Moreno 1955).

Although the linguistic differences between the speech described here and Common Somali might, in other political and cultural contexts, be sufficient to justify recognition of two distinct languages, I feel that the speech of Baydhaba should be regarded as a dialect of Somali until further study of the inter-relationship of the Central dialects has been completed.

While researching this article the author was supported by grants from the University of London and the School of Oriental and African Studies and enjoyed the facilities and hospitality of the National University of Somalia. The support of these institutions is gratefully acknowledged. I would like to thank the students of Lafoole College for their help and encouragement, particularly Shuayb and Abdulahi Jumaale. Thanks are also due to B. W. Andrzejewski for kindly allowing me access to his field notes on this dialect and to Nicky McDonald for her helpful comments.

2. PHONOLOGY

2.1. The phonemic inventory

The following is a list of the distinctive sounds of Central Somali. Each sound is represented in the table by its major allophone narrowly transcribed in the symbols of the I. P. A.[2] The inventory is followed by a key relating the I. P. A. symbols to the typographically simpler symbols used in this article to represent the phonemes.

		BIL.	LABIO-DENT.	DENT.	ALV.	POST-ALV.	PAL.-ALV.	PAL.	VEL.	UV.	GLOTTAL
CONSONENTS	Plosive + voice	b		d		$ɖ$		$ɟ$	g	G	
	− voice			t^h					k^h		$ʔ$
	Fricative + voice										h
	− voice		f		s		$ʃ$				
	Affricate + voice						$d̠ʒ$				
	Nasal	m			n			$ɲ$			
	Lateral				l						
	Tap				$ɾ$						
	Semi-vowel	w						j			
VOWELS	short	$ɪ$	$ə$	$ʊ$	long			$i:$		$u:$	
		$e̥$	$ɒ$	o				$e:$	$ʋ:$	$o:$	

---

[2] As described in *The Principles of the International Association*, London, 1949.

TRANSCRIPTION KEY

In the following key the lefthand symbols are those used in this article while the symbols to the right in the square brackets are the I. P. A. symbols for the major allophones.

b	[b]	s	[s]	e	[e̞]
d	[d]	sh	[ʃ]	a	[ɒ]
t	[tʰ]	j	[d̠ʑ]	ə	[ə]
ḍ	[ɖ]	h	[h]	u	[ɵ]
ɟ	[ʒ]	m	[m]	o	[o]
g	[g]	n	[n]	ii	[iː]
k	[kʰ]	ɲ	[ɲ]	ee	[eː]
q	[ɢ]	w	[w]	aa	[ɒː]
ʾ	[ʔ]	y	[j]	oo	[o]
f	[f]	i	[ɩ]	uu	[uː]

2.2. Notes on the phonemes

2.2.1. Phonological rules

Much of the variation from the major allophones given above may be generalized into several phonological rules. The most important of these seem to be weakening and assimilation:

WEAKENING
There seem to be two processes of weakening. The first is the intervocalic spirantization of voiced plosives, which as the following examples show, become homorganic voiced fricatives.

b → β	waraab	[wɒɾɒːβə]	'hyena'
d → ð	gadedi	[gɒðeðɩ]	'he bought it'
g → ɣ	magaar	[mɒɣɒːɾ]	'skin'

This process also affects geminates, reducing them phonetically to a single voiced plosive. In these cases the fricative versus plosive contrast takes over the phonological distinction between single and double consonants, e.g.

aabud	[ɒːβɵd]	'worship!'
aabudi	[ɒːβɵðɩ]	'he worshipped'
aabuddi	[ɒːβɵdɩ]	'she worshipped'

The other weakening process is the devoicing of voiced plosives when they occur finally in a word, e.g.

b → b̥	liib [liːb̥]	'lizard'	liibiyaal [liːβɩjɒːl]	'lizards'
d → d̥	heed [heːd̥]	'eagle'	heedo [heːðo]	'eagles'
g → g̥	lug [lɵg̥]	'leg'	lugo [lɵɣo]	'legs'

The voiced/voiceless plosive oppositions d/t and g/k are neutralized in this word final position.

ASSIMILATION

Assimilation as it affects nasals is discussed below. (2.2.2.). Aside from nasals, three types of assimilation are very prominent. Firstly there is assimilation between consonants in manner of articulation, e.g.

$$ul \quad + \quad t^ə \quad \rightarrow \quad ull^ə \qquad\qquad \text{'the stick'}$$
stick   the

$$maal \quad + t \quad + \quad i \quad \rightarrow \quad maalli \quad \text{'she milked it'}$$
milk   she   past

Secondly there is assimilation between homorganic plosives to agree in voicing. The definite article suffix provides good examples of this:

bad 'ocean'   -tə 'the'   baddə 'the ocean'
unug 'son'   -kə 'the'   unuggə 'the son'

Lastly there is nasalization of vowels. Whenever a syllable ends in a nasal stop, the preceding vowel is nasalized, e.g.

gamuun   [gɒmũːŋ]   'arrowshaft'
okumo   [okʰõ̃mo]   'eggs'
wan   [wɒ̃ŋ]   'milk'

2.2.2. Nasals

Nasal sounds present some difficulties for phonematization because of their widespread assimilation. In initial position in words three nasal sounds appear:

ɲ   e.g.   ɲaawduur   'wildcat'
n   e.g.   naag   'woman'
m   e.g.   malay   'fish'

and the same three sounds occur intervocalically:

ɲ   e.g.   maaɲə   'sea'
n   e.g.   unug   'son'
m   e.g.   rumaayi   'he believed it'

There are several contexts, however, where only one nasal may occur, and in most cases this can be seen as the result of assimilation to the place of articulation of the following sound, e.g.

m /−b   e.g.   shimbir   'bird'
n /−t, d   e.g.   wantə   'the milk'
ŋ /−k, g   e.g.   naŋkə   'the man'

However assimilation does not seem a likely factor in the word-final position, where only ŋ may occur, e.g.

shaŋ 'five'   waŋ 'milk'   aaŋ 'eat!'

The best approach seems to be to recognize three significant nasal sounds, ɲ, n and m, and two phonological rules which they obligatorily undergo:

P. R. 1   C   →   [α place]   / — C
                        [+nasal]   [α place]

P. R. 2   C   →   [+velar]   / — #
                        [+nasal]

The first rule informally describes the assimilation of nasals to a following consonant's place of articulation, and the second, the apparently more idiosyncratic constraint that word final nasals must be velar nasals. Note that the second rule suggests that different nasal phonemes may underlie this word-final velar nasal; this is supported by patterns such as the following:

naŋ	'man'	*namo*	'men'
sabeeŋ	'ewe'	*sabeeno*	'ewes'

In the above, final ŋ corresponds to both the phonemes *m* and *n*, i.e. by the operation of P. R. 1:

*nam → naŋ   *sabeen → sabeeŋ

Since however, at this stage of analysis, it is not always clear what the underlying segment is, velar nasals are always transcribed as ŋ in this article.

2.2.3. /h/

This sound seems very unstable when it occurs word finally. It may occur as a glottal stop, or may be dropped altogether, e.g.

li or *liʾ*	'six'	*lihduŋ*	'sixty' (*lih+tuŋ*)
cf. *afar*	'four'	*afartuŋ*	'forty'

There seems little doubt about the phonemic status of this sound, however. It occurs normally in initial and intervocalic positions, e.g.

hal 'one'   *dohowi* 'he spoke'

and even in word-final position it is not necessarily reduced, e.g.

maskah 'brain'   *ruh* 'churn it!'

2.2.4. The glottal stop

The phonological status of the glottal stop is problematical. As noted above, it can occur as an allophone of *h*. It also seems that any word beginning with a vowel may be pronounced with an initial glottal stop, although this may be associated with emphasis and needs further investigation. It is clear, however, that omission of the glottal stop in these cases does not affect the meaning of the word, which suggests that it is not phonologically significant in the normal sense.

There is one word, however, from which the glottal stop may not be deleted: *baʾiid* 'oryx'. It may prove that the glottal stop is in this case epenthetic, inserted to separate two vowels under the language's phonotactic rules (see 2.4. below). Since, however, the Common Somali cognate, *biciid* [bɪʕiːd], has a corresponding voiced pharyngeal, which is not epenthetic and which does not occur in this dialect, it seems that explication of this example must await further study. For the present, the glottal stop is not taken to be phonologically significant.

2.2.5. ə

The question for this sound is whether it is a vowel phoneme or the result of reduction rules on other vowel phonemes. There are several ways in which ə is unlike other vowels: when it occurs finally, for example, it is often reduced to a whispered vowel (represented below by a raised vowel), or may be so reduced that it is only detectable by the release of the preceding sound, e.g.

farowgə → *farowgᵊ* → *farowg* 'the zebra'

The determiner in the above example is the non-remote definite article (see 3.3. below); in the remote definite article *-ki/-ti*, there is no such reduction:

farowgi → **farowgⁱ* → **farowg* 'the zebra'

A second differentiating factor is that ə unlike other vowels does not occur as a long vowel; this fact might be predicted by an analysis that treated ə as a reduced vowel.

The strongest counterargument is that ə can occur in a syllable which is prominent, i.e. which has high tone, and as the following examples show, when it does, the vowel has the same quality as in non-prominent syllables:

eelə́də	'the gazelle'	L H L
gerə́gə	'the giraffe'	L H L

In the above examples both low and high tone examples of ə have the same vowel quality. This undercuts a reduction analysis of ə, since lack of stress would seem a likely trigger for such reduction and hence the high tone occurrences of ə above would have no obvious source. A conservative approach is adopted here: ə is recognized as a phoneme until stronger counterevidence comes to light. Nonetheless, it is interesting to note that this vowel corresponds to several different vowels in Common Somali cognates, e.g.

	COMMON SOMALI	CENTRAL SOMALI	
'time'	*beri*	*berə*	*i—ə*
'river'	*webi*	*wəbə*	*e—ə*
'the woman'	*naagta*	*naagtə*	*a—ə*
'dwarf antelope'	*sagaaro*	*sagaarə*	*o—ə*

2.3. Length

Both geminate consonants and long vowels are phonologically significant, as in Common Somali, e.g.

GEMINATION

booddə́	'flea'	*boodə́*	'thigh'
wéddi	'she drove it'	*wédi*	'he drove it'
máalli	'she milked it'	*máali*	'he milked it'

VOWEL LENGTH

shíid	'grind it!'	*shid*	'light it!'
hoorə́	'nomadic house'	*horə*	'before'
buur	'mountain'	*búr*	'flour'

2.4. Phonotactics

The following phonotactic rules have been observed:

1. Consonant clusters may only occur intervocalically, i.e. words may not begin or end with consonant clusters.
2. These consonant clusters are limited to two consonants.
3. Vowel plus vowel sequences, V V, do not occur, and rules operate to prevent them where they are predicted by some rule of the grammar (see below). Long vowels count as single vowels.
4. In the CC clusters combinations of most consonants may occur except that no voiceless plosives may close a syllable; hence, there are no voiceless geminates. Semivowels may only occur in the sequence semivowel + plosive.

An example of a rule operating to preserve the phonotactic constraints is vowel epenthesis. In the following examples, vowel + vowel sequences are predicted by the grammar; in each case an epenthetic glide *y* is inserted.

a.   *ilaali* + *i*   → *ilaaliyi*   'he looked after it'
           (root)   past

   cf.

        hir + *i*   → *hiri*   'he tethered it'
           (root)   past

b.   *Bayḍowə*   *ya*   *kə*   *kooyi* 'I came from Baydhaba'
           B.   focus   from   came

   cf.

        Hamar   *a*   *kə*   *kooyi* 'I came from Hamar'
           H.   focus   from   came

2.5.   Tone

2.5.1.   General

Central Somali has three phonological tones: a basic high tone versus low tone opposition and a high to low falling tone found over long syllables in some verb forms. Usually only one syllable has high tone, and all polysyllables were found to have one syllable with high tone, at least in the form found in isolation, which is taken here as the reference form.

This tone opposition could possibly be described in terms of accent or stress. Prominent syllables are higher in pitch, slightly longer than their non-prominent counterparts (whether short or long), and louder. Since, however, there seems to be at least one case where a syllable low in pitch is stressed (see 5.3. below, yes-no questions), the present study describes this prominence in terms of tone.

Phonetically there are three levels of pitch since before a pause low tones are lower than elsewhere, but since this is entirely predictable, this very low tone is taken as an allotone of the phonological low tone. In this article high tones are marked with an acute accent, *á* or *áa*; low tones are unmarked, *a* or *aa*; and high falling tones are marked as a grave accent, *àa*.

2.5.2. Tone in nouns

The following discussion deals with nouns in the form found in isolation, which is the general non-subject case. This is because although tone does seem to be involved in subject marking, e.g.

úsə díli	'he killed it'
usə́ díli	'it killed him'
he killed	

It is not yet clear how this subject marking interacts with the basic tone patterns described here.

2.5.2.1. Polysyllabic nouns

All nouns with three or four syllables have high tone on the last syllable. This syllable retains the high tone when a determiner is suffixed. This pattern is the same regardless of gender or vowel length, e.g.

ɖaɖaməsə́ (f)	'gecko'	ɖaɖaməsə́də	'the gecko'
kirkirə́ (m)	'wild pig'	kirkirə́gə	'the wild pig'
ɖilmaaɲə́ (f)	'mosquito'	ɖilmaaɲə́gə	'the mosquito'
sanjəbíil (m)	'ginger'	sanjəbíilkə	'the ginger'

Most disyllabic nouns show the same pattern, again regardless of gender:

osbə́ (f)	'salt'	osbə́də	'the salt'
gorgór (m)	'vulture'	gorgórkə	'the vulture'
boodə́ (f)	'thigh'	boodə́də	'the thigh'
aftíin (m)	'light'	aftíinkə	'the light'

There are a small number of disyllabic nouns which have a different pattern, that of high tone on the first syllable. These include both masculine and feminine nouns, e.g.

sériir (f)	'oil'	seríirtə	'the oil'
fárow (m)	'zebra'	farówgə	'the zebra'
ókun (f)	'egg'	okúntə	'the egg'
éyduur (m)	'wild dog'	eydúurkə	'the wild dog'

These patterns mean that masculine and feminine polysyllabic minimal pairs are not distinguished by tone, e.g.

aríir	'boy'	aríirko	'a boy'	aríirkaas	'that boy'
aríir	'girl'	aríirto	'a girl'	aríirtaas	'that girl'

2.5.2.2. Monosyllabic nouns

In both long and short monosyllables there is a regular correspondence between tone and gender: masculine nouns have high tone while feminine nouns have low, e.g.

MASCULINE

ɖúl	'earth'	ɖúlkə	'the earth'
búr	'flour'	búrkə	'the flour'
sóʾ	'meat'	sóʾkə	'the meat'
wéer	'jackal'	wéerkə	'the jackal'
móos	'banana'	móoskə	'the banana'
róob	'rain'	róobkə	'the rain'

FEMININE

bad	'ocean'	*baddə́*	'the ocean'
waŋ	'milk'	*wantə́*	'the milk'
lug	'leg'	*lugtə́*	'the leg'
heed	'eagle'	*heeddə́*	'the eagle'
buur	'mountain'	*buurtə́*	'the mountain'
jeer	'hippopotamus'	*jeertə́*	'the hippopotamus'

This correlation between tone and gender means that there are monosyllabic masculine and feminine minimal pairs distinguished by tone:

éey	'male dog'	*éeykə*	'the male dog'
eey	'female dog'	*eeytə́*	'the female dog'
wéel	'male calf'	*wéelkə*	'the male calf'
weel	'female calf'	*weellə́*	'the female calf'
wáar	'male kid'	*wáarkə*	'the male kid'
waar	'female kid'	*waartə́*	'the female kid'

For the rest of this article tone is only marked on nouns when it is unpredictable, i.e. on disyllabic nouns of the pattern HIGH-LOW.

2.5.3. Tone in verbs

In the verbal system each paradigm has a characteristic tone pattern. In the following examples some paradigm patterns are given for three verbs: a basic verb, *sumud* 'brand', and verbs with the radical extensions *-i* and *-oy*, *tiri* 'count' and *goroy* 'know' (see 4.1. below for discussion of these radical extensions). In each verb the paradigm pattern is the same:

PAST	*súmudi*	*tíriyi*	*górodi*
IMPER. SINGULAR	*sumúd*	*tirí*	*goróy*
IMPER. PLURAL	*sumudə́*	*tiriyə́*	*gorodə́*
NEG. IMPER. SINGULAR	*əŋ súmuddoy*	*əŋ tíriydoy*	*əŋ górotoy*
NEG. IMPER. PLURAL	*əŋ súmuddèen*	*əŋ tíriydèen*	*əŋ górotèen*

In some cases, due to the mechanics of root extension, these paradigm patterns distinguish homophonous verbal forms, e.g.

wáraabi	'he drank it'
waraabí	'water it!'
kári	'it boiled'
karí	'cook it!'

Usually, however, segmental features, i.e. endings, also distinguish each paradigm (see 4.3. below for details).

It must be noted that these verbal tone patterns seem very sensitive to variations in sentence intonation; it seems that the sentence final position is important in this respect. Unfortunately, it is not possible at the present stage of analysis to say anything substantive about this interaction between inherent verbal tone patterns and sentence intonation. It will be assumed in the rest of this article that verbs have the tone pattern characteristic of the paradigm exemplified in each case.

3. NOUN PHRASE MORPHOLOGY

3.1. Gender and number

The system of gender and number in nouns is complicated and the following description is forwarded as an initial approximation.

3.1.1. Gender

Gender and number may be isolated by two concord systems. The first is the agreement between the verb and its subject. In this there are three third-person patterns: masculine singular, feminine singular, and a common plural, e.g.

(1) *naŋkə sartuŋ   ɖisədaayə*   'the man who is building this house'
     man + the house + this build

(2) *naagtə   sartuŋ   ɖisədaaytə*   'the woman who is building this house'
     woman + the house + this build

(3) *shimbiro buulkuŋ   ɖisədaayaaŋ*   'the birds who are building this nest'
     birds   nest + this build

The second system involves the form of determiners and proforms triggered by nouns. Here there is a binary distinction between a set whose initial consonant is -*k* and one whose initial consonant is -*t*, e.g.

(4) *naŋkə* 'the man'   *naŋkuŋ* 'this man'   *naŋkaas* 'that man'   *naŋkee* 'which man?'
     ki kalə 'the other one'

(5) *naagtə* 'the woman'   *naagtuŋ* 'this woman'   *naagtaas* 'that woman'   *naagtee* 'which woman?'
     ti kalə 'the other one'

Since in the singular, -*k* proforms and determiners are triggered by nouns taking masculine verb concord, and -*t* forms by those taking feminine concord, it seems that both concord systems follow a masculine/feminine gender distinction in the singular.

This subcategorization is not stable when the noun becomes plural. Here the verbal concord is undifferentiated for gender, e.g.

(6) *naago sheeneeŋ*   'some women who brought it'
(7) *namo sheeneeŋ*   'some men who brought it'

While the -*k*/-*t* proform and determiner concord still identifies two sets or genders, a noun's plural form does not necessarily remain in the same set as its singular. One may take the two major forms of plural formation to demonstrate this:

(a) -*yaal* plurals

Many nouns seem to take a plural suffix -*yaal*, regardless of whether the singular noun belongs to the -*k* or -*t* set, e.g.

(7) *jeer*   'hippo'   *jeertaas*   'that hippo'   *jeeriyaal*   'hippos'
     shimbir 'bird'   *shimbirtaas*   'that bird'   *shimbiriyaal*   'birds'
     ba'iid   'oryx'   *ba'iidkaas*   'that oryx'   *ba'iidiyaal*   'oryxes'
     weer   'jackal'   *weerkaas*   'that jackal'   *weeriyaal*   'jackals'

These *-yaal* plurals all take the *-k* concord set, e.g.

(8) *jeeriyaalkaas*   'those hippos'
     shimbiriyaalkaas   'those birds'
     ba'iidiyaalkaas   'those oryxes'
     weeriyaalkaas   'those jackals'

If the *-k* set has been identified as masculine, then the following diagram describes the relationship between singular nouns and their *-yaal* plurals:

-YAAL PLURALS

SINGULAR   PLURAL

Masculine)
Feminine)   Masculine

(b) *-o* plurals

A large set of nouns take a plural suffix *-o*, again regardless of whether the singular noun belongs to the *-k* or *-t* set, e.g.

(9) *fileer* 'arrow'   *fileertaas*   'that arrow'   *fileero*   'arrows'
     laaŋ   'branch'   *laantaas*   'that branch'   *laamo*   'branches'
     shiid   'stone'   *shiidkaas*   'that stone'   *shiido*   'stones'
     eleeŋ   'ram'   *eleeŋkaas*   'that ram'   *eleemo*   'rams'

These *-o* plurals, unlike *-yaal* plurals, do not belong to a single *-k/-t* concord set; they display an interesting pattern of polarity: the plural noun belongs to the opposite set to that of its singular, e.g. (where intervocalic *-k* and *-t* become voiced)

(10) *fileerogaas*   'those arrows'
     laamogaas   'those branches'
     shiidodaas   'those stones'
     eleemodaas   'those rams'

If the *-k* and *-t* sets are identified as masculine and feminine, than the relationship may be represented diagrammatically thus:

-O PLURALS

SINGULAR   PLURAL
Masculine   →   Feminine
Feminine   →   Masculine

Note that if the singular noun consists of two short syllables then the *-o* plural is often reduced to two syllables, e.g.

(11) gebər   'girl'   gebro   'girls'
      habar   'old woman'   habro   'old woman'

There are several nouns which occur in both *-yaal* and *-o* plurals, e.g.

(12) qaansə   'bow'   qaansiyaal   'bows'   qaanso   'bows'
      shimbir 'bird'   shimbiriyaal 'birds'   shimbiro 'birds'

It is not clear whether these alternative plurals have different interpretations or are in free variation.

There is a third plural suffix which has been noted. This is *-iya*, whose occurrence seems to be phonologically conditioned: it only occurs when the singular noun ends in ə, e.g.

(13) makaawə   makaawiya   'bead(s)'
      inɖoolə   indooliya   'blind person(s)'
      buundə   buundiya   'bridge(s)'
      baaldə   baaldiya   'bucket(s)'
      birə   biriya   'buttock(s)'
      silsilə   silsiliya   'necklace(s)'
      shiidmarə shiidmariya 'grindstone(s)'
      farantə   farantiya   'ring(s)'
      yaambə   yaambiya   'hoe(s)'
      moorə   mooriya   'enclosure(s)'

It is difficult to ascertain whether this suffix involves polarity of gender since speakers seemed reluctant to accept forms with the definite article. There occurred, however, one example which seems to indicate that polarity is involved:

(14) ɖerə   'cooking pot'   ɖerəgə   'the cooking pot'
      ɖeriya   'cooking pots'   ɖeriydə   'the cooking pots'

Finally, the following idiosyncratic plural forms appear:

(15) ariir   'boy'   ariiɲo   'boys'
      dug   'old man'   dugoshin   'old men'
      kursə   'chair'   kuraas   'chairs'

In the present study the custom, normal in Cushitic studies, of identifying the *-k* and *-t* proform and determiner concord sets as masculine and feminine gender respectively, is followed.

3.1.2. Number

For the sake of clarity, in the discussion of gender above a simple singular/plural number system was assumed. In fact this dialect has a three way distinction between a general form which may be understood to refer to a set or one of its members, a singulative form which must refer to a single member of the set, and plural. The general form is morphologically simplest, being the noun's base form, i.e. it is unmarked, while singulative and plural forms involve suffixation onto that base form. Plural forms were discussed above in relation to gender, so the following examples show the contrast between general and singulative forms.

(16) naag   'woman'   naagto   'a woman'
      naŋ   'man'   naŋko   'a man'

| dab | 'fire' | dabko | 'a fire' |
| ɖar | 'cloth' | ɖarko | 'a cloth' |

Note that the singulative suffix is morphologically similar to the set of determiners (see 3.3. below).

3.2. Case

There seem to be two major case forms: a subject case and a general non-subject case. Subjects are differentiated from non-subjects by tone alone. The precise interaction between this case marking, word tone shape, and sentence intonation is as yet unclear. What is evident is that subject case is associated with a lowering of high tone, e.g. compare the nounphrases in (17) below:

(17) gurbí shéeni   'he brought a camel'
      gurbi shéeni   'a camel brought him'

      wéy ba shéeney naŋkɔ́   'he brought the man'
      wéy ba shéeney naŋkə   'the man brought him'

It seems that this subject case marking is neutralized when the subject is focused by the particle *a* (see 5.2. below), e.g.

(18) naŋkó wá shéeni   'it was a man who brought it'
      naŋkí yá shéeni   'it was the man who brought it'

All functional roles other than subject: object, indirect object, locatives (see 4.2.2.1.), etc. belong to one undifferentiated non-subject case, as do nouns uttered in isolation. This case is taken as the unmarked form.

3.3. Determiners

Apart from the singulative suffix described above (3.1.), the following sets of determiners occur. Each reflects the binary division into the -k/-t concord sets.

3.3.1. Definite article

There are two forms of definite determiner, -kə/-tə and -ki/-ti. The latter may be termed the remote definite article and the former the non-remote. If the referent is distant or in the past tense, the remote article is used while the non-remote is used for the opposite.
The latter seems to be more general in use, occurring whem the distinction is unclear or unimportant. The following are examples of this remote/non-remote distinction:

(19) naŋki   intə kə noolədə jəri meeluŋ   kə   tabi
      man + the here in live   used place + this from went

      'the man who used to live here has moved away'

(20) naŋkə   intə kə noolə askarwə
      man + the here in live   soldier + is

      'the man who lives here is a soldier'

The noun phrase 'the man' is *naŋkə* in (20), but *naŋki* in (19).

3.3.2. Demonstratives

There are two demonstratives, *-kuŋ/-tuŋ* and *-kaas/-taas*, which again might be termed non-remote and remote, being translatable as 'this' and 'that' respectively. Examples of these are

(21) *daaɲeerkuŋ*   'this monkey'   *daaɲeerkaas*   'that monkey'
      shiriftuŋ   'this comb'   *shiriftaas*   'that comb'

3.3.3. Possessives

These are suffixes morphologically similar to other determiners. The full set is given below; again there are two forms, reflecting the gender of the base noun:

(22) *sartey*   'my house'   *gurbəgey*   'my camel'
      sartaa   'your (sg.) house'   *gurbəgaa*   'your (sg.) camel'
      sartiis   'his house'   *gurbəshey*   'his camel'
      sartiye   'her house'   *gurbəshee*   'her camel'
      sartaynə   'our house'   *gurbəgaynə*   'our camel'
      sartiinə   'your (pl.) house'   *gurbəgiinə*   'your (pl.) camel'
      sartiyo   'their house'   *gurbəsho*   'their camel'

cf.   *sartə* 'the house', *gurbəgə* 'the camel'

3.3.4. Interrogative determiner

Any noun can be questioned by the suffixation of the interrogative determiner, *-kee/-tee*. Examples of this are

(23) *habartee?*   'which old woman?'   *gurbəgee?*   'which camel?'

      meellee   kə   aamaanə?   'where shall we eat?'
      place + which   in   eat

3.4. Pronouns

3.4.1. Bound pronouns

There are no subject pronouns in Central Somali corresponding to Common Somali's *aan, aad, uu*, etc., 'I, you, he' etc. The only bound pronouns are the object pronouns, which as in Common Somali must occur immediately before the verb, as follows:

(24) 1   *i*   *i aragi*   'he saw me'
      2s   *kə*   *kə aragi*   'he saw you'
      3m   -   }
      3f   -   }   *aragi*   'he saw him/her/it'
      1p   *nə*   *nə aragi*   'he saw us'
      2p   *səŋ*   *səŋ aragi*   'he saw you (pl.)'
      3p   -   *aragi*   'he saw them'

Thus in this dialect, unlike Common Somali, sentences may occur without an overt subject, i.e. there being no bound subject pronouns; as the above examples show.

3.4.2. Free or emphatic pronouns

These are as follows:

(25)   1s   *anə*
       2s   *adə*
       3m   *usə*
       3f   *iyə*
       1p   *unnə*
       2p   *isəŋ*
       3p   *iyo*

These may occur as either subject or non-subject, their distribution paralleling full NPs. Their functional status, i.e. subject or non-subject, is marked as in other NPs by tone; compare the tone patterns of *usə* 'he/him' in the following examples:

(26)   *warsóy   haddí   iyə   fadóytə   intí   usə́   ároostə*
       ask   if   she   want   that   him   marry

       'ask her if she wants to marry him'

       warsóy   wallə́   usə   áragi
       ask   thing + the he   see

       'ask him what he saw'

These pronouns differ from Common Somali emphatic pronouns in two respects. Firstly, there is no inclusive/exclusive distinction in the 1st person plural: *nə* and *unnə* are unspecified as to whether the listener is included or not. Secondly, these pronouns do not seem to combine with the definite article as do Common Somali *aniga, adiga* etc., 'I, you' etc.

3.4.3. Other pronouns

There are two other pronouns, *lə* the unspecified person pronoun 'one' or 'someone', e.g.

(28)   *naŋkə   lə   dili*   'the man someone killed, the man who was killed'
       man + the   one   kill

and *əs,* the reflexive and reciprocal pronoun, which is invariable, e.g.

(29)   *əs   dili*   'he killed himself'
       self   kill

(30)   *mey ənəs   ga looynə?*   'why should we fight each other?'
       what for + each other   fight

3.5. Numerals

3.5.1. Cardinal numerals

The gender of the following numerals is given as either *m* for masculine or *f* for feminine.

(31) kow f   'one'   saddun   m   'thirty'
      lamə f   'two'   afartun   m   'forty'
      siddə f   'three'   kontun   m   'fifty'
      afar f   'four'   lihdun   m   'sixty'
      shaŋ f   'five'   todobaatun m 'seventy'
      liᶜ f   'six'   siyeetun   m   'eighty'
      todobə f   'seven'   sagaalun   m   'ninety'
      siyeed f   'eight'   boqol   m   'hundred'
      sagaal m   'nine'   lamə boqol   'two hundred'
      tomu m   'ten'   siddə boqol 'three hundred'
      labaataŋ m   'twenty'   kuŋ   m   'thousand'

In compound numerals tens are connected to units by *iyə* 'and', e.g.

(32) tomi iyə kow   'eleven'
      tomi iyə siddə   'thirteen'
      labaatiyə kow   'twenty one'

while hundreds and tens are unconnected, e.g.

(33) siddə boqol afartuŋ iyə shaŋ   'three hundred and forty five'

While *kow* 'one' is used in counting, when it quantifies a noun, 'one' is *hal*, e.g.

(34) hal naag   'one woman'

When a numeral quantifies a noun it precedes the noun and attracts the determiner:

(35) sagaal laŋ   'nine men'
      sagaalkə laŋ   'the nine men'

The quantified noun, as the above examples show, remains in the singular form.

3.5.2. Ordinal numerals

These are formed from the cardinal numerals by the suffixation of *-aad*, e.g.

(36) kowaad   'first'   siddəhaad   'third'
      lamaad   'second'   afaraad   'fourth'
      etc.

When these numerals qualify a noun they occur to the right of the noun, e.g.

(37) naag lamaad   'a second woman'

and they do not attract the determiner:

(38) naagtə lamaad   'the second woman'

This means that they cannot occur alone and must qualify a proform or other NP, e.g.

(39) ti lamaad 'the second one' (fem.)   ki lamaad 'the second one' (masc.)

These facts suggest that, unlike cardinal numerals, ordinal numerals may be adjectives and that the *-aad* suffix may be a category changing derivational affix.

3.6. Adjectives

Adjectives follow the noun and its determiners, and within the noun phrase, do not occur with a copula in the present tense, e.g.

(40)   *laŋ wiiŋ*   'a big man'
       laŋkə wiiŋ   'the big man'

       laŋ gaabaŋ   'a short man'
       laŋkə gaabaŋ   'the short man'

It seems justifiable to treat the above as relative clauses despite the lack of copula since in the past tense the reduced copula is evident:

(41)   *laŋki wiinaayi*   'the big man, the man who was big'
       laŋki gaabnaayi   'the short man, the man who was short'

Adjectives cannot occur alone; they must follow a noun or pronoun:

(42)   *ki wiiŋ*   'the big one'
       ki yar   'the small one'

In main sentences the adjectives occur with a reduced and suffixed copula as in the past tense relative clauses above, e.g.

(43)   *usə   ɖeeryə*   'he is tall'
       he   tall + is

       usə   ɖeeraayi   'he was tall'
       he   tall + was

4.   VERBAL MORPHOLOGY

In the following description the reference form for verbs is the imperative singular form, since this is usually homonymous with the root.

4.1. Verb classes

4.1.1. Inflectional classes

The principle inflectional classification of Common Somali verbs, that into weak and strong verbs (Andrzejewski 1964, 1968, 1975b), has apparently no counterpart in Central Somali. There are four verbs in Common Somali which display the "strong" pattern of vowel change in the root and prefixed person markers; these are (in 3rd masc. sg. past tense) *yidhi* 'say', *yimi* 'come', *yiil* 'be', *yiqiin* 'know'. Their counterparts in Central Somali (in corresponding forms) are *eri, koyi, yaali*, and *kasi*, respectively.

These like all Central Somali verbs are "weak" in that they mark tense changes and person by suffixation.[3] No strong form verbs were encountered. It is possible to classify the verbs on inflectional patterns, but this, as described in the next section, must be based indirectly on the system of derivational affixes.

4.1.2. Derivational classes

As in other Cushitic languages there is in Central Somali a system of root extensions which can modify the meaning of a verb's root. The two main extensions are a causitive, or transitivizing, affix and a reflexive, or autobenefactive, affix. The relationship between a basic verb and its modified counterparts is not always simple, as will appear. Some roots do not occur in all three possible forms, or even in two, while in other cases the semantic relationship between two forms is less than transparent. These extensions do not have a constant phonological shape throughout a verb's paradigms and so for convenience the morph which occurs in imperative singular forms will be chosen as the reference form. A discussion of these extensions follows.

4.1.2.1. The causative/transitive extension

The reference form for this affix is *-i* or *-ey*. This extension has two main functions. If the base form is intransitive, the modified form is transitive, e.g.

(44)	*roog*	'stop, stay'		*rooji*	'cause to stop' (← **roogi*)
	kar	'boil (intrans.)'		*kari*	'cook'

If the base form is a transitive verb, the modified verb has a causative interpretation, e.g.

(45)	*waraab*	'drink' ·		*waraabi*	'water (animals)'
	ḍal	'give birth'		*ḍali*	'father, sire'
	kah	'rise'		*kahi*	'raise'

4.1.2.2. The reflexive/autobenefactive extension

This affix has the form *-oy* or *-ow* in the imperative singular. Its principal interpretation is autobenefactive, i.e. "for oneself", e.g.

(46)	*ḍis*	'build'		*ḍisoy*	'build for yourself'
	sheen	'bring'		*sheenoy*	'bring for yourself'

This may be suffixed to forms already modified by the causitive extension, and here it has the form *-soy*:

(47)	*waraabi*	'water'	*waraabisoy*	'water for yourself'
	rooji	'stop (trans.)'	*roojisoy*	'stop for yourself'

This extension may also carry a reflexive interpretation:

(48)	*bar*	'teach'		*baroy*	'learn'
	kahi	'raise'		*kahoy*	'get up'

---

[3]With the possible exception of the copula, which has different rootvowels in the present and past tenses. See 4.4.2. for comments.

In some cases the modification is less transparent:

(49)   *jiif*   'sleep'   *jiifoy*   'go to sleep'
       gad   'sell'   *gadoy*   'buy'
       roog   'stay, be in a place'   *roogsoy*   'stand up'

In both this and the causitive extension there are modified verbs for which the simpler forms have not been found, e.g.

(50)   *suubi*   'make'   *ilaali*   'look after'
       ɖimoy   'die'   *goroy*   'know, understand'

4.1.2.3. Other derivation affixes

The above extensions must be distinguished from other affixes found in verbs which, unlike the above, are category changing. Two important such affixes are *-aw* and *-ooy*. The first has the effect of forming a verb from the corresponding adjective, e.g.

(51)   *wiiŋ*   'big'   *wiinaw*   'become big'
       yar   'small'   *yaraw*   'become small, shrink'
       ɖeer   'tall'   *ɖeeraw*   'grow tall'
       gaabaŋ   'short'   *gaabanaw*   'become short'
       edaaŋ   'white'   *edaanaw*   'become white'

The second suffix, *-ooy*, is suffixed to nouns to form a related verb:

(52)   *waŋ*   'milk'   *wanooy*   'put milk into'
       biyə   'water'   *biyooy*   'put water into'
       sokor   'sugar'   *sokorooy*   'put sugar into'
       usbə   'salt'   *usbooy*   'put salt into'

These extensions differ from the root extensions in that they maintain their phonological shape in each paradigm. The root extensions have different reflexes in different paradigms, e.g.

(53)   *ɖis*   'build'   *ɖisoy*   'build for yourself'
       where the extension is *-oy*
       ɖisi   'he built it'   *ɖisidi*   'he built it for himself'
       where the extension is *-id-*

This means that, through a verb's paradigms, a modified verb will differ from a basic verb in a number of different ways. It is convenient to group verbs into three classes on the basis of their differences in any given paradigm. This resembles an inflectional classification but is based on the derivational affixes.

The classes are as follows: Class 1 will include verbs having the basic root form; Class 2, forms with the *-i* extension; and Class 3, verbs with the *-oy* extension. The differences reflected in these classes can be seen in the paradigms given below (4.3.). Note that verbs formed by the category changing affixes *-aw* and *-ooy* pattern with Class 1 verbs and that combinations of the extensions *-i* and *-oy* act like Class 3 verbs.

4.2. Morpheme Sequence

4.2.1. Verb Morphemes

As mentioned above, all Central Somali verbs encountered correspond to Common Somali "weak" verbs. This means that a verb form may be described as a sequence of morphemes like the following:

root (+ extension) + person marker + tense marker

In fact, as shown below, while five persons are distinguished by verb forms, only three of these are distinguished by person markers alone:

PERSON MARKERS

1sg./3m.sg./3pl.	∅ i.e. no marker
2sg./3f.sg./2pl.	*-t-*
1pl.	*-n-*

The extra distinctions are made by the fact that in each paradigm the 2pl. and 3pl. person forms have a different form of the tense/aspect marker from other persons. This is shown below:

(54)   The five-fold person distinction

sheeni	'I/he brought it'
sheenti	'you/she brought it'
sheenni	'we brought it'
sheenteeŋ	'you (pl.) brought it'
sheeneeŋ	'they brought it'

The full seven person distinction is gained by adding the subject pronouns.

4.2.2. Pre- and post-verbal morphemes

Apart from the morphemes of the verb itself there are a number of morphemes associated with the verb and which might to a greater or lesser extent be treated as verb affixes. These are discussed below.

4.2.2.1. Locative particles

These are elements corresponding to prepositions and postpositions in other languages, and as the following examples show, they occur immediately before the verb rather than with a noun phrase:

(55) *Hamar   a   ku   koyi*   'I came from Hamar'
       H.   FOCUS   from   came

(56) *wey ba   ku   koyey   Hamar*   'I came from Hamar, it was Hamar I came from'
       FOCUS   from   came   Hamar

(57) *iddə gudaashe   laŋnə   mə   kə   jerin*
       house inside + its no one   NEG   in   was

       'Nobody was inside the house'

(58) *libeyaal*   *a*   *kə*   *jibadeen*   *moorədə*   *binaanshə*
      lions   FOCUS   in   roared   enclosure + the   outside + its

      (lit. 'lions roared in the enclosure's outside)   'Lions roared outside the enclosure'

Regardless of the position of their associated noun phrases, these particles occur immediately before the verb. A full list of the particles encountered is

(59) *ku*   'from, at'
      kə   'in, on, with (instrument)'
      əŋ   'for, to'
      lə   'with (comitative)'

It is not yet clear how fixed the relative order of these particles is, nor whether they can be separated from the verb by other elements. These factors will determine whether they should be treated as part of the verb or not. See Andrzejewski (1960) for a discussion of the corresponding elements in Common Somali.

4.2.2.2. Negative particles

These are the following:

1.   *mə*   main sentence negative particle

(60) *mə*   *sheennə*   'I didn't bring it'
      NEG   bring

2.   *əŋ*   subordinate clause negative particle

(61) *inti adun*   *adə*   *roogtə*   *wal hor*   *adə*   *əŋ*   *aragnə ya*   *lə*   *aragə*
      while world   you   stay   thing before   you   NEG   see FOCUS   one   see

      (lit. 'while you remain in the world, a thing you have not seen before will be seen')
      (proverb) 'As long as you live you will see new things.'[4]

3.   *əŋ*   negative imperative particle

(62) *əŋ gaddoy*   'Don't sell it (sg.)!'
      əŋ gaddee   'Don't sell it (pl.)!'

Once again these particles seem bound to the verb; the only elements which seem able to occur between them and the verb are the locative particles described above, as example (57) above shows.

4.2.2.3. Yes-No question suffix

Finally, there are the elements suffixed to verbs to form yes-no questions. These are discussed below (see 5.3.) but do seem to be genuinely suffixed to the verb, e.g.

(63) *iyo*   *qosoleenaa ?*   'Did they laugh?'   *iyo*   *qosoleeŋ*   'They laughed'
      they   laugh + Q

---

[4]This example was kindly provided by Dr. B. W. Andrzejewski (personal communication).

(64)   *jebtey ?* 'Did it break?'   *jebti*   'it broke'
       break + Q

4.3. Paradigms

The following are the main sentence verbal paradigms which have been encountered.[5] For each paradigm the following verbs have been chosen as examples: *sheeŋ* 'bring' (Class 1), *tiri* 'count' (Class 2), and *goroy* 'understand, know' (Class 3).

1. Habitual present tense: "I bring"

	C1	C2	C3
1sg.	*shéenə*	*tíriyə*	*górodə*
2sg.	*shéentə*	*tíriydə*	*górotə*
3m	*shéenə*	*tíriyə*	*górodə*
3f	*shéentə*	*tíriydə*	*górotə*
1pl	*shéennə*	*tíriynə*	*góronnə*
2pl	*shéentaaŋ*	*tíriydaaŋ*	*górotaaŋ*
3pl	*shéenaaŋ*	*tíriyaaŋ*	*górodaaŋ*

The negative forms for this tense are marked by the particle *mə* and by a change from LOW to HIGH-FALLING tone on 2pl and 3pl endings, e.g.

      mə shéenàaŋ 'they do not bring it'

2. Simple past tense: 'I brought,' 'I have brought'

	C1	C2	C3
1sg	*shéeni*	*tíriyi*	*górodi*
2sg	*shéenti*	*tíriydi*	*góroti*
3m	*shéeni*	*tíriyi*	*górodi*
3f	*shéenti*	*tíriydi*	*góroti*
1pl	*shéenni*	*tíriyni*	*góronni*
2pl	*shéenteeŋ*	*tíriydeeŋ*	*góroteeŋ*
3pl	*shéeneeŋ*	*tíriyeeŋ*	*górodeeŋ*

The negative for this tense is a single invariable form, preceded by *mə*, e.g.

      mə sheennə 'I/you/he/she/we/etc. did not bring it'

---

[5] Subordinate clause verb forms are differentiated from main sentence forms. The mechanics of the system are still unclear but, for example, the subordinate forms of the near future tense paradigm are very similar to the main sentence negative forms of the same tense, e.g.

      fade   'he wants it/will want it'
      məfadaw   'he doesn't want it/won't want it'

3. Near future tense: 'I am about to bring it'

	C1	C2	C3
1sg	sheené	tíriyé	gorodé
2sg	sheenáasə	tíriyáasə	gorodáasə
3m	sheené	tíriyé	gorodé
3f	sheenáasə	tíriyáasə	gorodáasə
1pl	sheenáanə	tiriyáanə	gorodáanə
2pl	sheenáasaŋ	tíriyáasaŋ	gorodáasaŋ
3pl	sheenáayaŋ	tíriyáayaŋ	gorodáayaŋ

The negatives for this tense are preceded by *mə*. In addition the high tone shifts to the root vowel and 1sg and 3m endings become *-aw*, e.g.

> *mə tíriyaw*   'I am not about to count it'
> *mə tíriyaasə*   'she is not about to count it'

4. Future tense: 'I will bring it'

	C1	C2	C3
1sg	sheenə dóonə	tiri dóonə	gorodə dóonə
2sg	sheenə dóontə	tiri dóontə	gorodə dóontə
3m	sheenə dóonə	tiri dóonə	gorodə dóonə
3f	sheenə dóontə	tiri dóontə	gorodə dóontə
1pl	sheenə dóonnə	tiri dóonnə	gorodə dóonnə
2pl	sheenə dóontaaŋ	tiri dóontaaŋ	gorodə dóontaaŋ
3pl	sheenə dóonaaŋ	tiri dóonaaŋ	gorodə dóonaaŋ

As can be seen from the above, this is one of several tenses which involve auxiliary verbs; the main verb occurs in an invariable form while concord is marked on the auxiliary. Here the latter is *doon* (Class 1), which is in the inflectional pattern of the habitual present tense. In Common Somali this verb *doon* means 'to wish, want'; in Central Somali, however, this verb does not seem to occur as a main verb, its place being taken by *fad* (C1) 'wish, want'.

Negatives in this and all tenses which use an auxiliary are characterized by *mə*, which precedes the main verb, and the auxiliary appearing in the appropriate negative form. Since here *doon* is in the present habitual tense it forms negatives as in 1. above, e.g.

> *mə sheenə dóonə*   'I will not bring it'

Thus tenses with auxiliaries have no independent negative forms.

5. Present continuous tense: 'I am bringing it'

	C1	C2	C3
1sg	sheenə háayə	tiri háayə	gorodə háayə
2sg	sheenə háaytə	tiri háaytə	gorodə háaytə
3m	sheenə háayə	tiri háayə	gorodə háayə
3f	sheenə háaytə	tiri háaytə	gorodə háaytə
1pl	sheenə háaynə	tiri háaynə	gorodə háaynə
2pl	sheenə háaytaaŋ	tiri háaytaaŋ	gorodə háaytaaŋ
3pl	sheenə háayaaŋ	tiri háayaaŋ	gorodə háayaaŋ

Here again the auxiliary verb *haay* (C1) is in the habitual present tense and again is not found as a main sentence verb, although it may be related to *laháay* (C1) 'have'. As shown below, reduced forms of this tense are also found. Both variants seem to be used but speakers claim that the fuller forms are more characteristic of the speech of Baydhaba while the reduced forms are more common in the Bur Hakaba area.

	C1	C2	C3
1sg	*sheenóoyə*	*tiriyóoyə*	*gorodóoyə*
2sg	*sheenóoytə*	*tiriyóoytə*	*gorodóoytə*
3m	*sheenóoyə*	*tiriyóoyə*	*gorodóoyə*
3f	*sheenóoytə*	*tiriyóoytə*	*gorodóoytə*
1pl	*sheenóoynə*	*tiriyóonə*	*gorodóonə*
2pl	*sheenóoytaaŋ*	*tiriyóoytaaŋ*	*gorodóoytaaŋ*
3pl	*sheenóoyaaŋ*	*tiriyóoyaaŋ*	*gorodóoyaaŋ*

In each case alternative forms occur in which the long penultimate vowel *-oo-* is replaced by *-aa-*, e.g.

   sheenáayaaŋ   'they are bringing it'

These alternatives seem to be in free variation.

i)	C1	C2	C3
1sg	*sheenə háayi*	*tiri háayi*	*gorodə háayi*
2sg	*sheenə háayi*	*tiri háayti*	*gorodə háayti*
3m	*sheenə háayi*	*tiri háayi*	*gorodə háayi*
3f	*sheenə háayti*	*tiri háayti*	*gorodə háayti*
1pl	*sheenə háayni*	*tiri háayni*	*gorodə háayni*
2pl	*sheenə háayteeŋ*	*tiri háayteeŋ*	*gorodə háayteeŋ*
3pl	*sheenə háayeeŋ*	*tiri háayeeŋ*	*gorodə háayeeŋ*

ii)	C1	C2	C3
1sg	*sheenáayi*	*tiriyáayi*	*gorodáayi*
2sg	*sheenáasi*	*tiriyáayi*	*gorodáasi*
3m	*sheenáayi*	*tiriyáayi*	*gorodáayi*
3f	*sheenáasi*	*tiriyáasi*	*gorodáasi*
1pl	*sheenáani*	*tiriyáani*	*gorodáani*
2pl	*sheenáaseeŋ*	*tiriyáaseeŋ*	*gorodáaseeŋ*
3pl	*sheenáayeeŋ*	*tiriyáayeeŋ*	*gorodáayeeŋ*

Here the auxiliary, again *haay* (C1), is in the simple past form, and the same observations about the distribution of full and reduced forms hold. It is interesting that the person marker *-t-* becomes *-s-* in the reduced forms.

7. Conditional tense: 'I would bring it'

	C1	C2	C3
1sg	*sheenə laháayi*	*tiri layáayi*	*gorodə laháayi*
2sg	*sheenə laháayti*	*tiri laháayti*	*gorodə laháayti*
3m	*sheenə laháayi*	*tiri laháayi*	*gorodə laháayi*
3f	*sheenə laháayti*	*tiri laháayti*	*gorodə laháayti*
1pl	*sheenə laháayni*	*tiri laháayni*	*gorodə laháayni*
2pl	*sheenə laháayteeŋ*	*tiri laháayteeŋ*	*gorodə laháayteeŋ*
3pl	*sheenə laháayeeŋ*	*tiri laháayeeŋ*	*gorodə laháayeeŋ*

This paradigm has *laháay* (C1) 'have' which does occur as a main verb (see 4.4. below). Here it appears in the simple past tense form.

8. Past habitual tense: 'I used to bring it'

	C1	C2	C3
1sg	*sheenə jéri*	*tiri jéri*	*gorodə jéri*
2sg	*sheenə jérti*	*tiri jérti*	*gorodə jérti*
3m	*sheenə jéri*	*tiri jéri*	*gorodə jéri*
3f	*sheenə jérti*	*tiri jérti*	*gorodə jérti*
1pl	*sheenə jérni*	*tiri jérni*	*gorodə jérni*
2pl	*sheenə jérteeŋ*	*tiri jérteeŋ*	*gorodə jérteeŋ*
3pl	*sheenə jéreeŋ*	*tiri jéreeŋ*	*gorodə jéreeŋ*

The auxiliary in this paradigm is *jer* (C1) 'be, exist' which occurs normally as a main verb. Here it is in the simple past tense form.

9. Optative: this paradigm has the interpretation 'let him bring it!', 'may he bring it!'. The second person forms do not occur, suggesting that this paradigm might be in complementary distribution with the imperative.

	C1	C2	C3
1sg	*sheenóy*	*tiriyóy*	*gorodóy*
2sg	–	–	–
3m	*shéenoy*	*tíriyoy*	*górodoy*
3f	*shéentoy*	*tíriydoy*	*górotoy*
1pl	*shéennoy*	*tíriynoy*	*góronnoy*
2pl	–	–	–
3pl	*shéeneeŋ*	*tíryeeŋ*	*górodeeŋ*

10. Imperative: 'Bring it!'

		C1	C2	C3
	2sg	*sheen*	*tiri*	*goróy*
	2pl	*sheenə́*	*tiriyə́*	*gorodə́*
Negative:	2sg	*əŋ shéentoy*	*əŋ tíriydoy*	*əŋ górotoy*
	2pl	*əŋ shéentèeŋ*	*əŋ tíriydèeŋ*	*əŋ górotèeŋ*

4.4. Irregular verbs

There are two verbs which differ substantively from the patterns described above: they are *laháay* 'have' and the copula. These are described below.

4.4.1. *laháay* 'have'

The following forms have been observed for this verb:

1. Present tense: 'I have'   Negative: 'I do not have'

1sg	*lahá*		1sg	*mə lihi*
2sg	*letɔ́*		2sg	*mə lihid*
3m	*leyɔ́*		3m	*mə lə*
3f	*letɔ́*		3f	*mə lə*
1pl	*lennɔ́*		1pl	*mə lihiiŋ*
2pl	*létiiŋ*		2pl	*mə lihidiiŋ*
3pl	*léyiiŋ*		3pl	*mə lə*

2. Past tense: 'I had'   Negative: 'I did not have'

This is one invariable form: *mə ləhayn*

1sg	*laháayi*
2sg	*laháayti*
3m	*laháayi*
3f	*laháayti*
1pl	*laháayni*
2pl	*laháayteeŋ*
3pl	*laháayeeŋ*

4.4.2. The copula

It is interesting to note the difference above between present tense *laha* 'I have' and the rest of the paradigm. This difference in the root, suggesting perhaps partial suppletion, is paralleled in the present tense of the copula, shown below.

1sg	*áha*	'I am'	1pl	*énnə*	
2sg	*étə*		2pl	*étiiŋ*	
3m	*éyə*		3pl	*éyiiŋ*	
3f	*étə*				

The root variation in *laháay* is *lah~le* and in the copula, *ah~e*. In the copula, suppletion is clearly evident since there are alternative forms oí the present tense for all but first person singular:

1sg	*ahá*	'I am'	1pl	*háayni*	
2sg	*háayti*		2pl	*háayteeŋ*	
3m	*háayi*		3pl	*háayeeŋ*	
3f	*háayti*				

e.g. *eey éyə?* ⎫
      eey háayi ⎭ 'who is he?'

Note that these alternative forms closely parallel the auxiliary verbs in present continuous and past continuous tenses, and further, that they appear to be a cognate of the Common Somali verb *haay* 'have'. The other observed forms of the copula are as follows:

2. Present tense negative		3. Past tense: 'I was'	
1sg	*mə ihi* 'I am not'	1sg	*aháy*
2sg	*mə ihid*	2sg	*aháyti*
3m	*mə eh*	3m	*aháy*
3f	*mə eh*	3f	*aháyti*
1pl	*mə ihiŋ*	1pl	*aháyni*
2pl	*mə ihidiiŋ*	2pl	*aháyteeŋ*
3pl	*mə eh*	3pl	*aháyeeŋ*

4.4.3. Verbless sentences

In third person "equational" sentences of the form 'A is B', the copula does not occur, but is replaced by the particle *wə*, e.g.

(65)   *gurbə́wə*   'it's a camel'
        camel + *wə*

(66)   *Ali askárwə*   'Ali is a soldier'
            soldier + *wə*

In similar Common Somali sentences, e.g.

(67)   *awr weeye*   'it's a camel'

(68)   *Cali askari weeye*   'Ali is a soldier'

the element *weeye* can be seen as a reduced form of the combination of *waa*, the verb focus particle (Andrzejewski 1975a) and the copula. The problem for a similar approach to Central Somali *wə* is that there is no overt verb focus particle to parallel Common Somali's *waa* (see 5.2. below for discussion of this) and hence apparently no source for *wə*. Given that there is little phonological justification for identifying a phonologically null labio-velar glide -*w*- followed by a reduced copula, the status of *wə* must for the moment remain problematic. This suffixed particle can be reduced from *wə* to *u*, as in the following, when the preceding noun ends in a vowel, e.g.

(69)   /*gurba wə*/ → *gurbú*   'it's a camel'

For the present it is assumed that there is no overt copula in these sentences and that they provide the only instance in Central Somali of a corresponding particle to Common Somali *waa*.

5. SYNTAX

5.1. Word order

The usual sentence word order is S-(X)-V, where X is any non-subject noun phrase or combination of noun phrases. See for example the following instances of SOV order:

(70)   *bilaantə*   *hunguri*   *kariyaayaan*   SOV   'The women are cooking food'
        women + the   food   cook

(71) *idiyo*   *hoolǝ*   *mǝ*   *lǝ*   SOV   'their family does not have any livestock'
      family + their   livestock   NEG   have

The same sequence is displayed by the following examples, which have locative phrases composed of complex noun phrases of the form [NP - N+Poss]
                                                                                     NP

(72) *ŋaawtǝ*   *miiskǝ*   *hoostiis*   *a*   *kǝ*   *jertǝ*   S LOC V
      cat + the   table + the   beneath + its FOC   in   is

      'the cat is underneath the table'

(73) *hogollǝ*   *buurtǝ*   *korshe*   *ya*   *roogtǝ*   S LOC V
      cloud + the   mountain + the above + its   FOC   stay

      'the cloud is above the mountain'

Since the principal exception to this word order is Wh-questions (see 5.4. below), where other rules of the grammar operate to ensure that the questioned NP occurs leftmost, it seems reasonable to identify S-(X)-V as the basic word order.

Throughout this article there occur examples of the more detailed relative order of elements within the sentence. These are here generalized into rules:

(1) Determiners are suffixed to the noun (3.3.)
(2) Relative clauses follow the head noun and its determiners (5.5.)
(3) Adjectives follow the noun (3.6.)
(4) Cardinal numerals precede the noun (3.5.1.)
(5) Ordinal numerals follow the noun (3.5.2.)
(6) Auxiliaries follow main verbs (4.3.)
(7) Locative particles precede the verb (4.2.2.1.)
(8) Bound object pronouns precede locative particles, e.g.

(74) */i + ǝŋ sheeg/* → *iiŋ sheeg*   'tell me!'
                  me + to tell

(9) Negative particles precede locative particles (4.2.2.1.:S57)

5.2. Focus

The means by which Central Somali sentence elements are marked as being focused show some similarity to focus marking in Common Somali. The basic uses of focus seem the same, including the introduction of new items into the discourse and the placing of contrastive stress. One useful test for focus is the aptness of replies to wh-questions; these entail specific requests for new information, and, as the examples below show, the replies must focus the new items. In the following, all the sentences are grammatical, the symbol * denotes an inapt reply.

(75)   a. *Abdi meν sheeni?*   'what did Abdi bring?'
        b. *Abdi besǝ ya sheeni*   'Abdi brought MONEY'
        c. **Abdi ya besǝ sheeni*   'ABDI brought money'

(76)   a. *eeν sheeni besǝdǝ?*   'who brought the money?'
        b. *Abdi ya besǝdǝ sheeni*   'ABDI brought the money'
        c. **Abdi besǝdǝ ya sheeni*   'Abdi brought THE MONEY'

NP focus is marked by the particle *(y)a* occurring immediately after the NP. Sentences (75c) and (76c) above are infelicitous because in them presupposed rather than new NPs are focused.

The focus particle has several phonological realizations, the determining factor apparently being the final sound of the preceding NP. If this is a consonant, the particle is *a*; if it is a vowel, or there is a pause, then the particle has an initial epenthetic glide, *-y-* after a pause or front and central vowels, and *-w-* after back vowels. Hence the form of the focus particle in the following:

(77)   *shaley*   *ya*   *kə*   *tabni*   'we left YESTERDAY'
        yesterday   FOC   from   went + we

(78)   *shaleyto*   *wa*   *kə*   *tabni*   'we left YESTERDAY'
        yesterday   FOC   from   went + we

(79)   *Hamar*   *a*   *əŋ*   *jeedə*   'I am going to HAMAR (Mogadishu)'
        H.   FOC   to   go + I

There is a second NP focus structure which occurs as an alternative to *a*. Whenever an NP focused by *a* is apt the structure *wey ba (Verb) NP* is also apt. Compare sentences (75) and (76) above with the following alternative forms:

(80)   a. *Abdi mey sheeni?*   'what did Abdi bring?'
        b. *Abdi wey ba sheeney besə*   'Abdi brought MONEY'

(81)   a. *eey sheeni besədə?*   'who brought the money?'
        b. *besədə wey ba sheeney Abdi*   'ABDI brought the money'

It seems likely that this is a cleft structure and that the most precise translation of (81b) above should be 'the one who brought the money is Abdi'. No examples have been found of NPs being marked by a focus particle in subordinate clauses nor of NPs inside complex NPs being focused. Note for example the focused NP in the following sentence:[6]

(82)   *lamə*   *laŋ*   *ya*   *arageeŋ*   'they saw two men'
        two   men   FOC   (they) see

This seems to correspond to both the English sentences:

They saw TWO MEN.
They saw TWO men.

In short, focus seems unable to pick out elements within a complex NP. In hierarchical terms, the focus particle may only be attached to the highest NP. i.e.

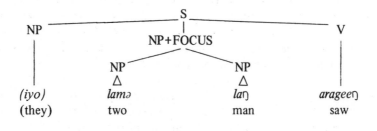

---

[6] I am assuming here that *lamə* is a normal NP, which seems to be the case.

In addition no examples have been found of two NPs being focused in the same sentence. It seems clear that *a* and *wey ba* correspond to Common Somali's *baa/ayaa* and *waxa* respectively. For verb focus, however, the correspondence is less exact. Common Somali has the particle *waa*, at least part of whose function is to mark focus on verbs (Andrzejewski 1975a). There is apparently no such particle in Central Somali. In environments where Common Somali *waa* would be predicted, there occur sentences without any overt focus particles. Compare, for example, (83) below in Common Somali with (84) below, its Central Somali counterpart:

(83)   a. *Cabdi*   *muxuu*   *ku*   *sameeyey*   *lacagtii ?*   'What did Abdi do with the money?'
          A.   what + he   with   did   money + the

         b. *wuu*   *xadáy*   'he stole it'
          waa + he stole

(84)   a. *Abdi*   *mey kə*   *subiyi besədə ?*   'What did Abdi do with the money?'
          A.   what with   did money + the

         b. *hadi*   'he stole it'
           stole

Thus in Central Somali, as example (84b) above shows, sentences may occur without a focus particle. Whether verb focus is involved in all such cases is not yet clear. Further examples of this particle-less verb focus are shown below:

(85)   a. *aragey?*   'did he see it?'
         b. *aragi*   'he saw it'
         c. *ḑimaadeenaa?* 'did they die?'
         d. *ḑimaadeen*   'they died'

5.3. Yes-no questions

Yes-no, or polar, questions are differentiated from declarative sentences by suffixation of elements to the sentence final constituent, the verb. The form of these suffixes depends on the verb ending: 2nd person plural and 3rd person plural endings, which end in -ŋ, have *-aa* suffixed while all other endings, which end in vowels, become *-ey*, e.g. *-i* → *ey* and *-ə* → *ey*. In addition there is a distinct sentence intonation associated with these questions: the corresponding declarative sentence's pitch relations, i.e. its "tune", are maintained but the whole is raised in pitch. Thus a phonologically low tone in a yes-no question may be as high in pitch phonetically as a phonologically high tone in a declarative sentence. The following are examples of declarative and question pairs, with the pitch phonetically marked for the first:

                       S   Q

(87)   *usɔ́*   *aróosə*   *doontə*   *usɔ́*   *aróosə*   *doontey ?*
       him   marry   will   him   marry   will + Q

       'she will marry him'   'will she marry him?'

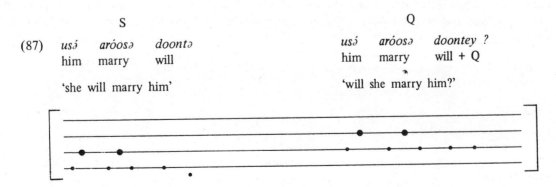

	S		Q	
(88)	*isiŋ díleeŋ*		*isiŋ díleenaa ?*	
	'you (pl.) killed it'		'did you (pl.) kill it?	
(89)	*jébti*		*jébtey ?*	
	'it broke'		'did it break?'	
(90)	*kasáayaaŋ*		*kasáayaanaa ?*	
	'they know it'		'do they know it?'	

Although the question suffix has low tone it is more stressed than low tone verb endings elsewhere. As discussed earlier (see 2.5.1.), low tones before a pause are phonetically lower than low tones in other contexts. This is accompanied by a falling off of intensity, or volume, and a shortening of syllable length. Yes-no question suffixes are an exception to this; as can be seen from the phonetic transcription of pitch in example (87) above, the usual drop in tone does not occur, nor is there any lessening of syllable length. This is interpreted here as stress.

Embedded yes-no questions, or indirect questions, are introduced in two ways: by *haddi* 'if' or by the normal subordinate clause complementizer *in/inti* 'that'. For the present the latter is treated as a separate element from the homonymous *in* (n. fem.) 'place; way, fashion'.[7]

The following are examples of these embedded questions:

(91) | *wey ba* | *fadoy inti* | *ogaadə in* | *Ali hiraabtuŋ* | *shaqeeyi* |
|---|---|---|---|---|
| FOC | (I) want that | (I) know *that* | A. morning + this | work |

'I want to know whether Ali worked this morning'

(92) | *mə* | *ogi* | *haddi* | *iŋglan* | *əŋ* | *jeedi* | *amə* | *ameerikə* |
|---|---|---|---|---|---|---|---|
| NEG | know | if | E. | to | went | or | A. |

'I don't know whether he went to England or America'

(93) | *warsoy* | *haddi* | *iyə* | *fadooytə* | *inti* | *usə* | *aroostə* |
|---|---|---|---|---|---|---|
| ask (her) | if | she | want | that | him | marry |

'ask her if she wants to marry him'

5.4. Wh-questions

Wh-questions are marked by the presence of a questioned NP. This can be of two types: a noun with a wh-determiner "which, what?", e.g. *meellee?* 'which place?', or one of a limited series of question words whose internal structure is not so clear, e.g. *eey?* 'who?'. These wh-words seem to have "built-in" focus since they occur in sentences where the verb is presupposed and thus unlikely to be focused, yet where no NP focus particle occurs, e.g.

(94) | *eey* | *ruuntə* | *sheegi ?* | 'who told the truth?'
|---|---|---|
| who | truth + the | told |

---

[7]If they are treated as the same items then all sentential complements, i.e. *that*-clauses, will be relative clauses on the lexical item *in.*

These words usually occur leftmost in the sentence, e.g.

(95)   *mey   laŋkə   əŋ   tumə   haayaaŋ ?*   'why are they beating the man?'
       what   man + the   for   (they) are beating

but may be preceded by certain elements which seem to be topics, e.g.

(96)   *shaahi   eey   kariyə ?*   'the tea, who makes it?'
       tea + the   who   cook

The noun phrase *shaahi* in the above seems to be a topic for several reasons: there may be a substantial pause between it and the sentence; omitting it leaves a grammatical sentence; and finally, this shorter sentence is apt wherever the longer version can be used.

Wh-question words do not occur in subordinate clauses. As the examples below show, indirect wh-questions are relative clauses headed by non-interrogative NPs, e.g. main sentence *eey?* 'who?' is paralleled by *naŋkə* 'the person', *mey?* 'what?' by *wallə* 'the thing', *mey ... əŋ?* 'what for, why?' by *sababtə* 'the reason'. The following show the major wh-words and their corresponding subordinate clause NPs:

1. *mey?* 'what?'

   Main sentences:

   (97) *mey fadaasə?*   'what do you want?'
   (98) *mey aragi?*   'what did he see?'
   (99) *mey subyaanə?*   'what shall we do?'

   Subordinate clauses:

   (100) *iiŋ   sheeg   wallə   usə   fadaw*   'tell me what he wants!'
          me + to   tell   thing + the he   want

   (101) *warsoy   wallə   usə   aragi*   'ask him what he saw!'
          ask (him)   thing + the he   saw

   (102) *eey   kasə   wallə   unə   suubyaanə?*   'who knows what we will do?'
          who   know   thing + the we   shall do

2. *eme?* 'when?'

   Main sentences:

   (103) *eme kooyaasə?*   'when are you coming?'
   (104) *eme ḍimadi?*   'when did he die?'
   (105) *eme jiifadaayaaŋ?*   'when do they sleep?'

   Subordinate clauses:

   (106) *walbə   mə   dibaw   marki   adə   kooyaasə*
          nothing   NEG   be   difficult time + the you come

          'it doesn't matter when you come'

   (107) *marki   ḍimadi gorədaasey?*   'do you know when he died?'
          time + the   died   (you) know + Q

(108)   *weydi*   *marki*   *jiifadaaŋ*   'ask them when they sleep'
        ask (them)   time + the   sleep

3.   *eey ?* 'who?'

Main sentences:

(109)   *eey aragti ?*   'who did you see?'
(110)   *eey fade ?*   'who does he want?'
(111)   *eey guursadaasə ?*   'who will she marry?'

Subordinate clauses:

(112)   *gorədaanə*   *naŋkə*   *aragti*   'we know who you saw'
        (we) know   person + the   (you) saw

(113)   *iiŋ*   *sheeg*   *naŋkə usə*   *fadaw*   'tell me who he wants'
        me + to   tell   person + the   he wants

(114)   *mə*   *sheegaasə*   *naŋkə*   *guursadə doontə*
        NEG   (she) will tell   person + the   (she) marry will

        'she won't say who she will marry'

4.   *intee ?* 'where?'

Main sentences:

(115)   *intee əŋ jeeddə ?*   'where are you going?'

(116)   *intee*   *kə*   *dalati ?*   'where was she born?'
        place + wh   in   born

(117)   *intee*   *kə*   *aamaanə ?*   'where shall we eat?'
        where   in   we eat

Subordinate clauses:

(118)   *gorodə*   *meellə*   *adə*   *əŋ*   *so'otə*
        (I) know   place + the   you   to   go

        'I know where you are going'

(119)   *weydi meellə*   *kə*   *dalati*   'ask her where she was born'
        ask (her) place + the   in   born

(120)   *adə*   *goosədaasə meellə*   *unə*   *kə*   *aamaanə*
        you   will decide place + the   we   in   will eat

        'you'll decide where we eat'

5. *mey ... əŋ ?*   'what for, why?'

Main sentences:

(121) *mey əŋ bahaasə ?*   'why are you leaving?'
(122) *mey əŋ ooyaasi ?*   'why was she crying?'
(123) *mey əŋ dagaaləmaanə ?*   'why should we fight?'

Subordinate clauses:

(124) *iiŋ   sheeg   sababtə   əŋ   bahooytə* 'tell me why you are leaving'
       me + to   tell   reason + the   for   leave

(125) *sababtə   əŋ   ooyooyti ya   ogtə*
       reason + the   (she) for   cry   FOC   (you) know

       'you know why she was crying'

(126) *laŋnə   miniiŋ   sheenə   sababtə   əŋ   dagaaləmaanə*
       no one   NEG + us + to   told   reason + the   for   (we) fight

       'no one told us why we should fight'

6. *sidee ?* 'how?' 'which way?'

Main sentences:

(127) *sidee eyə ?*   'how is he?'
(128) *sidee əŋ safari ?* 'how did he travel?'

(129) *sidee   əŋkə   meelluŋ   noolədaanə ?*   'how can we live in this place?'
       how   in + in   place + this   live

Subordinate clauses:

(130) *weydi   sidi   usə   eyə*   'ask him how he is'
       ask (him) way + the   he   is

(131) *wey ba   iiŋ   sheegey   sidi   əŋ   safari*
       FOCUS   me + to   told   way + the   in   traveled

       'he told me how he had traveled'

(132) *niiŋ   sheeg sidi   meeluŋ   iŋkə   tabə   lahaayni*
       us + to   tell way + the   place + this   in   leave   should

       'tell us how we should leave this place'

5.5. Relative clauses

Relative clauses, like all subordinate clauses, are differentiated from main sentences by the form of the verb, e.g. cf. (133) and (134):

(133)   *shaahi   ya   fade*   'I want tea'
        tea   FOC   (I) want

(134)   *wallə   anə   fadaw   shaahiwə*   'what I want is tea'
        thing + the   I   want   tea + is

Relative clauses have the characteristic order of head noun followed by the clause; there is no proform within the restricting clause, e.g.

(135)   *kuriyeerigi   Hamar   əŋ   jeedə   bahi*   'the bus which goes to Hamar has left'
        bus + the   H.   to   goes   left

(136)   *naŋki   intə   kə   noolədə   jeri   meeluŋ   kə   tabi*
        man + the   here   in   live   used   place + this away   went

        'the man who used to live here has left (here)'

As mentioned above (5.2.) focus particles do not occur in the relative clause. This may be for semantic reasons, i.e. that the content of a relative clause is generally presupposed and therefore unlikely to be focused. This would not, however, explain the absence of focus particles from other clauses; it may be that there is a more general constraint against focus marking which operates over all clauses.

5.6. Other clauses

5.6.1. Sentential complements

Sentences which function as subjects or objects of other sentences are introduced by the complementizers or nominalizers *in* or *inti*. It is not yet clear what factors determine the choice of one over the other.
Like all NPs such sentences may be focused by *a* or *wey ba*, e.g.

(137)   *wey ba   fadaase   inti   usə aroostə*   'she wants to marry him'
        FOCUS   (she) wants   that   (she) him marry

After the complementizer, these sentences have the same word order as main sentences:

(138)   *in   Ali   hiraabtuŋ   shaqeeyey   ogtaa ?*   ... S-NP-V ...
        that   A.   morning + this worked   know + Q

5.6.2. Other clauses

Other clause types encountered include the following temporal and conditional clauses. It remains to be seen whether these clauses are further instances of relative clauses. Similarly it is not clear whether *inti* in sentence (140) is the same element as the complementizer described above, or a defined form of the noun *in* (n. fem.) 'place; amount; way; time'.

(139)   *haddi   adə   koytə wey ba   kə   siyə   lahaayey   hunguri*
        if   you   come FOCUS (I)   you   give   would   food

        'if you come, I will give you food'

(140) *inti   usə   əmbannə   gee   kastə   aragə   jeri*
that(?)   he   left   day   every   (I) see   used

'before he left, I used to see him every day'

(141) *hoobə   usə   aragi   bahi*   'when he saw it, he left'
time   he   saw   (he) left

(142) *marki   diyaar   nagaanə ya   bahaanə*
time + the   ready   become FOCUS   (we) will leave

'when we are ready, we will leave'

6. VOCABULARY

In this vocabulary the following abbreviations are used, n: noun; a: adjective; v: verb; m: masculine, f: feminine; 1, 2, 3: verb classes (see 4.1.).

abdomen	*ukur* nm	birth, assist at	*ḍali* v2
add	*kə dar* v1	bitter	*qaraar* a
alcohol	*kamrə* nf	bitter	*midow* a
afternoon	*galab* nf	bladder	*kaadəgaleeŋ* nm
angry, become	*ḍirif* v1	blind person	*inḍoolə* nm
ankle	*qoob* nm	blood	*ḍiig* nm
ant	*ḍuur* nf	boil (intrans.)	*kar* v1
anus	*ḍusuŋ* nf	boil (trans.)	*karkari* v2
arm	*galaŋ* nf	bone	*laf* nf
arrow	*fileer* nf	bow	*qaansə* nf
around	*wareeg* n	boy	*ariir* nm
arrowshaft	*gamuuŋ* nm	bracelet	*jijiŋ* nf
ashes	*bedəmbed* nm	braid hair	*dab* v1
aunt, maternal	*ahayar* nf	brain	*maskah* nf
aunt, paternal	*inaay* nf	brand animals	*sumud* v1
avenge	*aargudoy* v3	bread	*gibis* nf
		bread, pancake type	*anjeerə* nf
back, upper (of body)	*irid* nf	break	*jeb* v1
back, lower (of body)	*duud* nm	breed animals (trans.)	*rimi* v2
bad	*huŋ* a	breakfast	*afbilaaw* nf
bad, become	*humaw* v	breast	*naas* nm
banana	*moos* nm	bridge	*buundə* nm
bead	*makaawə*	bring	*sheeŋ* v1
bed	*sareer* nf	bucket	*baaldə* nm
believe	*rumaay* v1	build	*ḍis* v1
belt	*suuŋ* nm	bury	*duug* v1
big	*wiiŋ* a	buttock	*birə* nf
bird	*shimbir* nf	bull	*dibə* nm
birth, give	*ḍal* v1	butter	*burud* nm
		buy	*gadoy* v3

calf, of leg	*kub* nm		dance	*ḍeel* v1
calf, male	*wéel* nm		darkness	*mugdə* nm
calf, female	*weel* nf		daughter	*gebər* nf
camels (collectively)	*gaal* nf		day	*gee* nm
camel, adult male	*gurbə* nm		day after tomorrow	*berə dambə*
camel, adult female	*hal* nf			n phrase m
camel, group of males	*uur* nf		day before yesterday	*shalaalədey*
camel, young male	*nirig* nm		deaf person	*ḍegoolə* nm
camel, young female	*nirig* nf		deep	*mool* a
camel, half-grown male	*waallə* nm		defecate	*haar* v1
camel, half-grown female	*jeer* nf		die	*ḍimoy* v3
cat, male	*ɲaaw* nm		difficult	*kakəŋ* a
cat, female	*ɲaaw* nf		dik-dik	*sagaarə* nf
cattle	*loʾ* nf		dirty	*wasak* a
chain	*silsilə* nf		divide	*qaybi* v2
chair	*kursə* nm		divorce	*fur* v1
cheetah	*mugshibeel* nm		dog	*eey* nm or f
chest, of body	*hibid* nm		door	*elbaab* nm
chicken, general	*doorə* nf		draw (water)	*dar* v1
chicken, cock	*diig* nm		dress	*guntoy* v3
chicken, hen	*doorə* nf		drink	*waraab* v1
chicken, half-grown	*boojal* nf		drive	*wed* v1
chicken, chick	*jijow* nm		drive out	*foofi* v2
child	*ariir* nm		dryness	*enjeg* n
children (collectively)	*eyaal* nm		dry season, lesser	*deer* nf
chili	*basbaas* nm		dry season, greater	*jilaal* nm
churn	*ruh* v1		dust	*bus* nm, *seegə* nf
circumcise	*gud* v1			
clay	*ḍoob* nf		eagle	*heed* nf
clean	*nadiif* a		ear	*ḍeg* nf
clitoris	*kintir* nm		earth, ground	*ḍul* nm
cloth	*ḍar* nm		earth, soil	*ʾarə* nf
cloud	*hogol* nf		easy	*fudud* a
cold	*qobow* a		eat	*aaŋ* v1
comb	*shirif* nf		egg	*ókuŋ* nf
come	*koy* v1		eight	*siyeed* nf
cooking pot	*ḍerə* nm		eighty	*siyeetuŋ* nm
cousin, maternal	*inaay* nm or f		elbow	*husul* nm
cousin, paternal	*inaadeer* nm or f		elder	*dug* nm
copulate	*korkor* v1		elder brother	*aboow* nm
count	*tiri* v2		elder sister	*abaay* nf
countryside, bush	*duur* nm		elephant	*maroodə* nm
countryside, cultivated	*adablə* nm		eleven	*tomiiyə kow*
countryside, open	*baŋ* nm			n phrase
cow	*saʾ* nf		emaciated	*baahə* a
crocodile	*yéhaas* nm		enclosure	*moorə* nf
cut	*gooy* v1		enclose (with a fence)	*mooroy* v3

enemy	*adow* nm	go	*bah* v1, *əŋ jeed* v1
evening	*fiid* nm	goats (collectively)	*eeriŋ* nm
eye	*il* nf	goat, male	*eesaŋ* nm
eyebrow	*hiddor* nm	goat, kid	*waar* nm or f
eyelash	*hirrib* nf	goatskin	*magaar* nm
eyelid	*baar* nm	good	*fayləŋ* a
		grain store	*bakaar* nf
fall	*rid* v1	granddaughter	*ariiti ariitiye* n phrase
far	*ḍeer* a	grandfather	*aboow* nm
fat	*adiiŋ* nf	grandmother	*abaay* nf
fat	*shilis* a	grandson	*ariiki ariishe* n phrase
father	*aaw* nm	graze	*daag* v1
feather	*bool* nm	graze, put to	*daaɟi* v
ferment	*eedag* v1	grind	*shiid* v1
few	*yar* a	grindstone	*shiidmar* nm
fifty	*kontuŋ* nm	ground squirrel	*tukuluush* nm
finger	*far* nf	grow	*kor* v1
fingernail	*iddə* nf	guinea fowl	*kabarey* n
fire	*dab* nm		
first	*kowaad* a	hair	*tiŋ* nf
firstborn son	*urud* nm	half	*nuus* nm
fish	*malay* nm	hand	*galaŋ* nf
five	*shaŋ* nf	hard	*adag* a
flat	*fidsin* a	hate	*kahoy* v3
flea	*booddə* nf	head	*madə* nm
flour	*bur* nm	hear	*kaalmey* v1
fly (insect)	*teesə* nm	heart	*widnə* nm
food	*hungurə* nm	hearth	*jikə* nf
foot	*kaab* nf	heel	*irib* nf
ford	*gow* nm	help	*kaalmey* v1
forearm	*ḍuḍuŋ* nm	hide (skin)	*megid* nf
forest	*ɟig* nf	hide, piece of	*jaaŋ* nf
forty	*afartuŋ* nm	high	*kor* nm
four	*afar* nf	hippopotamus	*jeer* nf
fourth	*afaraad* a	hobble (tie legs)	*dabar* v1
friend	*jeel* nm	hoe	*yaambə* nf
frog	*raaʾkə* nm	hoof	*qoob* nm
fry	*dub* v1	horn	*gaas* nm
fur	*duf* nf	hot	*kuleel* a
future	*koytə* nf	house, nomadic	*hoorə* nm
		house, stone	*sar* nf
gazelle	*eelə* nf	hump, camel's	*kurus* nm
gecko	*ḍaḍaməsə* nf	hump, cow's	*tuur* nf
ghee (clarified butter)	*ḍaaysə* nm	hundred	*boqol* nm
ginger	*sanɟəbiil* nm	husband	*laŋ* nm, *naŋ* nm
giraffe	*gerə* nm	hyena	*waraabə* nm
girl	*gebər* nf		

intestines	*manḍeer* nf	measure	*miisaŋ* v1
iron	*bir* nf	meat	*soʾ*
issue of same father	*iskə aaw* n phrase	men (collectively)	*rag* nm
issue of same mother	*iskə aay* n phrase	milk	*maal* v1
		milk	*waŋ* nf
jackal	*weer* nm	milk, fresh	*waŋ mey* n phrase
		milk, after a few hours	*mupə* nm
kidney	*kilə* nf	milk, camel's several hours	
kill	*dil* v1	after *mupə* stage	*soosə* nm
kindle	*shid* v1	milk, cow's after	
kinsman	*qaraabə* nf	fat extraction	*guruur* nf
kite (bird)	*huunfey* nf	milk, sour	*ḍanaaŋ* nm
knee	*jilib* nm	milk, fermented	*faddə* nm
knife	*tuurə* nf	milk container, large	*goloŋ* nf
know	*kas* v1	milk container, small	*bukur* nf
kudu	*dirdir* nf	mix	*kə qas* v1
		money	*besə* nf
lake	*qaydar* nm	monkey	*daaɲeer* nm
laugh	*kood* v1	monitor lizard	*gáanuug* nm
leather	*magaar* nm	month	*bil* nf
leave	*kə bah* v1	moon	*bil* nf
leaves	*hambal* nf	morning	*salaad* nf
leopard	*shibeel* nm	morning, early	*hiraab* nf
leg	*lug* nf	mortar	*moog* nm
light	*aftiiŋ* nm	mosquito	*dilmaaɲə* nf
like, love	*jeelow* v3	mother	*aay* nf
lineage	*abtir* nm	mountain	*buur* nf
lion	*libe* nm	mouse	*weləŋwelə* nf
lip	*faroor* nf	mouth	*af* nm
listen	*ḍugunsoy* v3	mud	*deegə* nf
liver (body)	*taraaw* nf		
liver (food)	*beer* nm	narrow	*iig* a
lizard	*libow* nm, *liib* nm, *abuur* nf	navel	*ukur* nm
loincloth	*keeraŋ* nm	near	*ḍow* a
look	*firi* v2	neck	*qoor* nf
louse	*injir* nf	necklace	*silsilə* nf
low	*hoos* nf	neck-rest	*barshiŋ* nm
low (cattle)	*weer* v1	new	*usub* a
low (camel)	*bərood* v1	night	*hamiiŋ* nm
lung	*sambab* nm	nine	*sagaal* nm
lynx	*mug* nf	ninety	*sagaaluŋ* nm
		nobody	*laŋnə*
mad	*waalaŋ* a	noon	*duhur* nm
make	*suubi* v2	nose	*saŋ* nm
man	*laŋ* nm, *naŋ* nm	nostril	*dul* nm
many	*badaŋ* a		
marry	*aroos* v1	ocean	*bad* nf

oil	*sériir* nf	sad, be	*ḍerif* v1
old	*dug* a	sand	*dooyə* nf
old, become	*dogow* v1	sandal	*kob* nf
old man	*dug* nm	salt	*osbə* nf
old woman	*habar* nf	say	*er* v1
one	*kow, hal*	say a poem	*gobey* v2
onion	*basal* nm	scarf, woman's	*haboog* nf
oryx	*baʾiid* nm	scream	*qaylə ḍaami* v2
ostrich	*goroɲə* nf	sea	*maaɲə* nf
		second	*lamaad* a
palm	*ḍanə* nf	see	*arag* v1
penis	*shuf* nf	seven	*todobə* nf
pepper	*filfil* nf	seventy	*todobaatuŋ* nm
person	*laŋ* nm, *naŋ* nm	sew	*tol* v1
pestle	*kal* nf	shallow	*bohol* a
pigeon	*anɟarə* nf	sheep (gen.)	*idə* nf
plant	*tilaal* v1	sheep (collectively)	*idaaley* nf
plough	*fal* v1	sheep, ram	*eleeŋ* nm
plough	*fal* nm	sheep, ewe	*sabeeŋ* nf
pound	*tuŋ* v1	sheep, lamb	*magal* nf
pour	*shub* v1	sheep and goats (coll.)	*eeriŋ* nm
precipice	*hoobud* nm	shield	*gaashaŋ* nm
pregnant, become	*uurow* v1	shirt, woman's	*ambuur* nm
pregnant, make	*uurey* v2	short	*gaabaŋ* a
pubic hair	*shuuŋ* nm	shortness	*gaab* nm
put on	*saar* v1	shoulder	*garab* nm
python	*ɟibisə* nm	shout	*qayli* v2
		sick, be	*jiroy* v3
rain	*roob* nm	sing	*hees* v1
rain	*roobooyi* v2	six	*liʾ* nf
rainy season, lesser	*ḍiddə* nf	sixty	*lihduŋ* nm
rainy season, greater	*guʾ* nm	skin	*kor* nm
rat	*jiir* nm	skin	*magaar siib* v1
reap	*gooy* v1	sky	*ʾir* nm
recover (from illness)	*faaysoy* v3	skirt, men's	*kar* nm
red	*gaduud* a	slaughter	*goori* v2
remember	*hasuusoy* v3	sleep, go to	*ɟiifoy* v3
repeat	*kə nag* v1	sleep	*hundur* v1
replete, become	*ḍereg* v1	small	*yar* a
rhinocerous	*wigil* nf	smell (trans.)	*uri* v2
rib	*feer* nf	smile	*muusow* v3
rice	*beriid* nm	smoke (milk)	*ul* v1
ring	*farantə* nm	snake	*ḍij* v1
rise	*kah* v1	soft	*ɟiliŋ* a
river	*wəbə* nm	soil	*ʾarə* nf
river, dry	*bóhol* nf	sole, of foot	*kaab* nf
rope	*hadag* nm	son	*unug* nm
roundworm	*hisɟa* nm	soup	*fuud* nm

sour	*ḍanaaŋ* a	two	*lamə* nf
sow	*abuur* v1	udder	*labə* nm
speak	*dohow* v1	uncle, maternal	*abtə* nm
spear	*waraŋ* nm	uncle, paternal	*adeer* nm
spider	*ʾaarəʾaarə* nf	understand	*goroy* v3
star	*hiddig* nm	urinate	*kaadi* v2
steal	*had* v1		
stick	*ul* nf	virgin	*gaashaaŋ* nf
stomach	*alool* nf	vomit	*mantag* v1
stone	*shiid* nm	vulture	*gorgor* nm
stool	*gimbir* nf		
suck	*nuug* v1	wake up, get up	*kahoy* v3
sweet	*mayaaŋ* à	want	*fad* v1
sword	*bilaab* nm	wash	*ḍig* v1
sun	*ʾirə* nf	watch over	*ilaali* v2
		water	*biyə* nm, *bi* nm
tail	*dab* nm	water	*waraabi* v2
take	*qaad* v1	water container	*haaŋ* nf
take off	*kə qaad* v1	water pot	*kuud* nf
tall	*ḍeer* a	watering place	*dow* nf
tapeworm	*goreyaaŋ* nm	weep	*ooy* v1
taste	*ḍaḍami* v2	well	*eel* nm
ten	*tomu* nm	wet	*qoyaaŋ* a
termite	*aboor* nm	white	*edaaŋ* a
testicles	*raay* nf	wide	*bilaar* a
tether	*hir* v1	wife	*naag* nf
thigh	*boodə* nf	wild buffalo	*loogees* nf
thin	*hayeesə* a	wild cat	*ɲaawduur* nf
think	*fikir* v1	wild pig	*kirkirə* nm
third	*siddəhaad*	wind	*dabeel* nf
thirteen	*tomiiyə siddə* n phrase	winnow	*heedi* v2
thirty	*sadduŋ* nm	wolf, wild dog	*éyduur* nm
thousand	*kuŋ* nm	woman	*naag* nf
three	*siddə* nf	women (collectively)	*bilaaŋ* nf
thresh	*shukul* v1	wood	*bileybar* nf
throat	*ḍuuŋ* nf	work	*shaqeey* v2
tie	*hir* v1	worship	*aabud* v1
time	*waqtə* nf	wrist	*miɟin* nf
tomorrow	*berə* n		
tooth-stick	*rumə* nm	year	*sinnə* nm, *sinnəd* nm
toe	*suul* nm	year, this	*sinnədkuŋ*
tongue	*anrab* nm	year, last	*sinnə horə*
tooth	*ilig* nf	year, next	*sinnə dambə*
tortoise	*diindiin* nm	yesterday	*shaley*
touch	*taaboy* v3	young man	*ḍalinyar* nm
truth	*ruŋ* nf		
twelve	*tomiiyə lamə* n phrase	zebra	*fárow* nm
twenty	*labaataŋ* nm		

BIBLIOGRAPHY

ANDRZEJEWSKI, B. W.

1960   "Pronominal and prepositional particles in Northern Somali." *African Language Studies* 1:96-108.

1964   *The Declensions of Somali Nouns.* London: School of Oriental and African Studies.

1968   "Inflectional characteristics of the so-called 'weak verbs' in Somali." *African Language Studies* 9:1-51.

1975a.   "The role of indicator particles in Somali." *Afroasiatic Linguistics* 1 (6):1-69.

1975b.   "Verbs with vocalic mutation in Somali and their significance for Hamitico-Semitic comparative studies." In James and Theodora Bynon (eds.), *Hamitico-Semitica*, pp. 361-367. The Hague: Mouton.

ARMSTRONG, L. E.

1934.   "The phonetic structure of Somali." *Mitteilungen des Seminars für Orientalische Sprachen zu Berlin* 37(3):116-161. [Reprinted in 1964 by Gregg Press, East Ridgewood, New Jersey]

LEWIS, I. M.

1955.   *Peoples of the Horn of Africa: Somali, Afar and Saho.* London: International African Institute. [Reprinted in 1969]

MORENO, M. M.

1955.   *Il Somalo della Somalia.* Rome.

REINISCH, L.

1904.   *Der Dschäbärtidialekt der Somalisprache.* Sitzungberichte der Kais. Akademie der Wissenschaften in Wien, Bd. 148, Heft 5. Vienna.

TILING, M. VON

1921/22. "Die Sprache der Jabarti, mit besonderer Berücksichtigung der Verwandtschaft von Jabarti und Somali." *Zeitschrift für Eingeborenensprachen* 12:17-52; 97-162.

1924/25. "Jabarti-Texte." *Zeitschrift für Eingeborenensprachen* 15:50-158.